a smart girl's guide to

knowing what to say

finding the words to fit any situation

by Patti Kelley Criswell

illustrated by Angela Martini

 ★ AmericanGirl®

Published by American Girl Publishing
Copyright © 2011 by American Girl

Questions or comments? Call 1-800-845-0005,
visit our Web site at americangirl.com,
or write to Customer Service,
American Girl, 8400 Fairway Place, Middleton, WI 53562.

Printed in China
12 13 14 15 16 17 18 LEO 10 9 8 7 6 5 4 3 2

Editorial Development: Trula Magruder, Jodi Goldberg, Kristi Thom
Art Direction and Design: Chris Lorette David
Production: Jeannette Bailey, Kendra Schluter, Tami Kepler, Judith Lary

Dear Reader,

Have you ever been stuck searching for the right words, but just couldn't find them? You felt yourself freezing up, forgetting, stuttering, or even hurting people's feelings without realizing it—or realizing it, but not knowing how to handle the situation in any other way.

It happens to everybody, but you can make it happen less often with a few simple tips, tricks, and tools— and a whole lot of practice!

Find a friend, a sister, a parent, or a mirror, and imagine yourself in one of the situations inside—we have more than 200—and practice using these words.

In no time at all, you'll be able to say exactly what you want to say when you need to say it, whether you're ordering in a restaurant, answering a question at school, or standing up for a friend. You'll learn the words to handle almost any situation—and you'll be able to speak with confidence and grace.

Your friends at
American Girl

contents

small talk

"We were just making small talk." This saying means the conversation was easy and light. With small talk, you're not sharing your deepest darkest secrets, but it's still an important part of everyday conversation. Small talk says that I want to know you better, that I care about you, and that what you say matters.

25 things to say after "hi"

Imagine that you want to start a conversation with the girl waiting next to you at the city bus stop, but you don't know what to say. After saying hi, try one of these questions to get the talk going.

1. I'm (your name). What's your name?
2. How's it going? 3. What school do you go to?
4. I'm in fifth grade. What grade are you in? 5. Do you take this bus often? 6. Do you ever bring an MP3 player to listen to?
7. Want to play a game while we wait? 8. Have you seen (the latest movie)? 9. I wish I had brought my book. Do you like to read? 10. Can you believe how (hot/rainy/cold) it is?
11. I thought I'd be late. Have you been here long?
12. So, what do you like to do when you're not waiting for buses?
13. Tonight (a TV show) is on. Do you ever watch that?
14. Would you like a piece of gum? 15. I have a ton of home-work. Does your teacher assign a lot of work? 16. I love your (something she's wearing). Is it your favorite color? 17. Do you know what time it is? 18. I can't wait for the weekend. I'm (give a detail about your plans). How about you?
19. I'm excited to get home to my new puppy. Do you have pets?
20. Have you lived here long? 21. I love your hair. Did you braid it yourself? 22. Want to sit together? 23. Do you think the bus will be late today? 24. Do you ride the school bus, too?
25. Where are you going today?

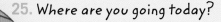

25 questions to know someone better

Now imagine that you've talked to this girl a few times before, and you think you have a lot in common. Try these questions to get to know her even better.

1. When is your birthday? 2. Have you ever tried out for a sport? 3. What's your favorite color? 4. Have you ever won anything? 5. Are you nervous about middle school? High school? 6. Do you like to cook? 7. Have you ever lived in a different state? Country? 8. Who is your favorite teacher? Why? 9. Do you collect anything? 10. What's your biggest fear? 11. Do you know what you want to be next Halloween? 12. Do you have any vacations coming up? 13. Where's your favorite place to hang out with your friends? 14. How many people are in your family? 15. Do you have a favorite singer? 16. Have you ever gotten lost? What did you do? 17. Do you have your own computer at home? 18. What's your favorite thing to do? 19. Do you have your own room? 20. What's your favorite TV show? 21. Do you have a dream job? 22. Do you like to ride on roller coasters? 23. Do you ever write poems or stories? 24. What kind of books do you like to read? 25. If you could live anywhere, where would it be?

when you're the new girl

Starting a conversation takes courage. But here's the thing—it only takes one sentence to get the talk going. So start with your name and an easy question. Then see where things go. It looks like this:

If you're new in school and want to meet girls at lunch: I'm Angela. How's it going? OK if I sit here?

If you just arrive at camp and walk in the cabin to find three sets of eyes staring at you: Hi! I'm Christina. So are the bunks first come, first served?

If your teacher puts you on a committee to choose library books: Hi, guys! I'm Olivia. I love to read, so this should be a lot of fun.

If you join a club, and you're asked to tell everyone a little about yourself: I'm Samantha, I'm 11, I have one sister, and I play the violin.

Take it slow. Never share private information until you know the person better.

Share your point of view

Sharing your thoughts, feelings, and opinions about things will help your friendship grow. By giving your point of view, you're letting others get to know you, and by speaking up, you're allowing your confidence to shine.

> I love the new school mascot! What do you think of the new colors?

> This is the best book I've read this year. I'd love to know what you think. Would you like to borrow it?

BIG IMPORTANT POINT

Part one of being confident is having a point of view. But part two is *really* caring about what others think. So after you've shared, invite others to share, too.

when someone else is new

Take the time to talk with someone new. If you've ever been "the new girl," you know how much it matters. So when you get the chance to brighten someone's day—take it.

If you want to meet a new girl, and she looks really shy:

Hi, I'm Bethany. Are you finding everything OK?

If you want to meet the new girl on the soccer team, but you're not sure what to say to her:

Hi, I'm Leigh. What position do you like to play?

If you want to invite the new girl to get together outside of school for the first time:

Do you want to go with me to the school carnival this weekend? It's always fun.

If you want to welcome a new girl to your scouting troop:

Hi, I'm Kasia. Today we're making raffia flowers. Would you like to sit with Ella and me?

If the new girl in class is assigned as your science partner:

Nice to meet you, Alex. Have you ever had to make invisible ink before?

Chitchatting Clues

Having a tough time getting the conversation started? Try this:
Look around you and find a person, place, or thing to talk about.
Now, strike up a conversation. Check out our examples.

when talking
with adults

Adults can be intimidating, but it's simple to make small talk if you really *listen* to what the adult is asking. Then add to the conversation with a bit more information or by asking a question.

If the uncle you haven't seen since you were a little kid asks, "What have you been doing for fun lately?"

Instead of this: "Not much."

Say this:
> I joined a travel soccer team—that's been fun. Mom said you went to Spain. What was that like?

If your great-aunt says, "Look how much you've grown!"

Instead of this: "I guess."

Say this:
> Yeah, I've grown out of my clothes this year. The doctor says I'm going to be taller than Mom.

If your friend's dad asks, "So what are you two hard at work on?"

Instead of this: "Homework."

Say this:
> Carly and I have to do homework about Mexico, so we're looking for pictures in these old travel magazines.

If you're waiting for class to start and your art teacher asks,
"Are you ready to make clay flowers today?"

Instead of this: "OK."

Say this:
> I'm excited. My mom has a flower garden, so I already have ideas that I want to try.

If a woman in your mother's book club sees you and asks,
"Gabriella, do you like to read?"

Instead of this: "Uh-huh."

Say this:
> I read all kinds of books, but I love graphic novels. Have you ever read one of those?

If your neighbor is working in her garden and asks,
"What have your parents been up to lately?"

Instead of this: "I don't know."

Say this:
> Mom's busy with work, and Dad's cleaning out the garage.

A TIP

When someone asks you a question, it's important that you say something other than "good" or "nothing." If you don't have much to say, ask a question. Questions help move the conversation back and forth like a ball in a tennis match—only in the end, you're both winners.

15

compliments

Admiring something about a person is a great way to start a conversation. It opens the door to even more talking and sharing. And who doesn't love a compliment? Check out these dos and don'ts when giving and receiving compliments.

GIVING compliments

- Do speak from the heart with honest and positive comments.
  Instead of this: "I liked your speech."

  Say this: *Your speech really kept my attention. You're a great speaker.*

- Do give specific details about what you like or liked.
  Instead of this: "Cool poem."

  Say this: *I loved your haiku, especially the line about your cat being a sushi specialist.*

- Don't expect a compliment back.
  Instead of this: "Nice sweater. Do you like mine?"

  Say this: *You look pretty in that sweater. It makes your eyes look so blue.*

- Don't add a "but" statement after complimenting someone.
  Instead of this: "Your party was fun, BUT my sister's party was amazing."

  Say this: *Your party rocked! I loved your decorations.*

RECEIVING compliments

- Do accept compliments with a sincere thank you.
  Compliment: "Your artwork is really cool."
  Instead of this: "Yeah, a lot of people have given me compliments."

  Say this: *Thank you! That means a lot to me.*

- Do give credit to a partner or partners if you receive a compliment on a group project.
  Compliment: "What a great project on recycling!"
  Instead of this: "Thanks!"

  Say this: *Thanks! I did the presentation, but Sophie and Natalie did most of the writing.*

- Don't agree in a bragging way.
  Compliment: "Another 100! You're so smart."
  Instead of this: "Yeah, I think it's easy to get all A's."

  Say this: *Thanks. I really like social studies.*

- Don't disagree or cut yourself down when receiving a compliment.
  Compliment: "Wow! You have an awesome voice."
  Instead of this: "Thanks, but I don't think I sang that well."

  Say this: *Thank you! I was nervous singing my first solo.*

17

confident body language

It's not just *what* you say but *how* you say it that matters. If you want to sound confident, you need to look the part. Negative body language can send signals that say you're not interested in talking. Follow these tips to show a potential friend that you're interesting and ready to be a part of her world.

Smile. Nothing makes a person feel more relaxed when he or she meets you than a welcoming smile. A smile tells a person that you have confidence in yourself.

Which of these two girls would you rather introduce yourself to?

Make eye contact. Looking someone in the eyes tells that person that you're interested in knowing her better. If you're not looking at the other person, she may think you're bored or want to be somewhere else.

Which of these two would you like to invite over to your house?

Relax your arms. As soon as someone walks up, relax your arms. If you fold your arms across your chest, you might send a signal that says you want that person to stay away from you. If you place your hands on your hips, you might look impatient or unfriendly.

Which of these girls would you like to ask to sit with you on the bus?

asking for what you want

Speaking up isn't always easy, but others can't help you if they don't know what you want. Begin by choosing a good place and time to talk. Then pair confident body language and a good attitude with a calm voice and the right words.

just say the word!

How do you rank when it comes to asking for what you want?
Take this quiz to find out.

1. Your family is going on vacation, and
   you'll have to miss a few days of school.
   You approach your teacher and say:

   a. **"My mom says you need to give me the
   work I'll miss."**

   b. **"Could I take some work with me to keep
   from getting too far behind?"**

   c. **Nothing.**

2. You don't get any playing time during the
   game, so you're frustrated and confused.
   You walk up to the coach and say:

   a. **"It's not fair! You keep putting in your
   favorite players."**

   b. **"Excuse me, Coach. I'd like to talk with
   you about my play time tonight."**

   c. **"Thanks. See you at practice."**

3. A friend asks you to come over to her
   house after the swim meet, but you're
   exhausted. You say:

   a. **"Ugh. I'm too tired."**

   b. **"I would love to, but can we do it
   another day? I'm so pooped that
   I wouldn't be any fun."**

   c. **"Sure."**

4. A girl you admire is running for student council, and you want to help her with her campaign. You say:

a. **"I'm your new campaign manager, OK?"**

b. **"I think you would be a great student council president. Do you want help with your campaign?"**

c. **"Good luck. Hope you win!"**

5. You want your best friend to come to your fancy recital, but you've never seen her wear anything but jeans. You say:

a. **"If you come, you gotta dress up. No one wears jeans."**

b. **"I hope you can make it to my recital. It's formal, but I'd love to help you find something fun to wear!"**

c. **Nothing. You hand her an invitation and hope she figures it out.**

Answers

Bulldozer
If you circled mostly a's, sometimes you can be too demanding. Tone down your approach, or you may find people avoiding you.

Blissfully Balanced
If you circled mostly b's, you know how to share what's on your mind without offending or embarrassing others. Your approach will get you through almost anything.

Barely Noticed
If you circled mostly c's, no one will be able to tell what you want or need—you're not telling! You find it hard to speak up, but if you don't, you'll end up feeling stomped on. Find your voice. Know that your bravery will be rewarded with less stress and more enjoyment in life.

if you want something from an adult

When talking with grown-ups, it's best to stick to the facts. Speak clearly (no mumbling!), be respectful, and state *exactly* what you need.

If the restaurant gets your order wrong:

> Excuse me, ma'am. I ordered the chicken and this is beef.

If the man at the movie concession stand looks scary, but you want to order:

> I'd like a small popcorn and a lemonade, please.

If you want to write a paper for class about your neighbor's career:

> Ms. Bello, I have a school project on careers, and I was hoping I could ask you a few questions about your job. What would be a good time?

If a teacher says, "I need a strong boy to carry this box," and you want to help:

> How about a strong girl? I'm willing to help out.

If you're invited to a friend's house for dinner, and you forget to say that you're allergic to dairy:

The mac and cheese looks great, but I can't have dairy. Sorry I forgot to tell you. May I have some extra fruit?

If you disagree with the grade you've received, and you want to talk to your teacher about it:

Mr. Howes, I'm confused by my grade. I thought I did the assignment exactly as you asked. Can you show me where I went wrong?

If you have to wait and wait and wait while the school secretary is on the computer completely ignoring you:

Excuse me. I'm sorry to bother you, but can you help me, please?

If your mom is late picking you up from practice, and your teammate's mom has a phone you need:

Hi, Mrs. McCormick. I was wondering if I could borrow your cell phone to call my mom?

about friendship troubles

Sometimes talking with a friend can get a little touchy, especially if you'd like her to stop doing something. When setting boundaries, be respectful, and reassure your friend that even though you don't like what she's doing, you still like her.

If you want friends to quit calling you by a nickname that you hate:

> Love you. Don't love the nickname. Could you stop, please?

If your friends start talking about a classmate they dislike, but you think they're being unfair:

> I'm not cool talking about this. Let's change the subject.

If your friend never brings money and always asks you to pay:

> I'm sorry, but I don't have any extra money to lend you today.

If a friend asks for some of your lunch after she's eaten her own:

> I don't usually bring extra, but if I do, you'll be the first to know.

If a friend keeps interrupting you to tell her own story:

> I want to hear your story, but let me finish first, OK?

if a friend makes you mad

Even best friends have disagreements. When a friend makes you mad, cool down before talking it out. It might be tough, but if you think things through, you'll have a better chance of working it out.

If you keep getting into trouble in class because a friend won't stop talking to you:

> Allie, I don't want to get in trouble, so I'm not going to talk during class. Unless we get some free time, I'll talk to you at lunch.

If a friend teases you in front of other people at school:

> I felt like you tried to embarrass me today, and I'm not happy about it. In fact, I'm pretty upset.

If a friend talks about you behind your back:

> I heard some really upsetting rumors, so we need to talk.

If a friend tells a secret that she swore never to tell:

> You broke my trust. I'm really mad, and I need time to calm down before we talk about it.

if you want parents to make a change

Asking parents to change the way they've always done something isn't easy. Below are some examples of common requests made by girls. If you've asked your parent for something in a respectful way, and they aren't convinced—turn the page.

If you want your mom to stop buying clothes that you feel are too old-fashioned:

I really appreciate that you thought of me, Mom, but I don't feel right in these clothes. Can we return them and look for something we both like?

If you want to choose your own hairstyle at the salon so that you don't end up with the same old look:

Thanks for taking me to get my hair cut. I'd really like a change. Can we look at a different style?

If you want your dad to quit taking over your school projects:

I know you're trying to help, Dad, but this needs to be my work or I can't turn it in. Can we work on a non-school project together?

If you want your parents to stop barging into your room

Can we agree to knock on each other's bedroom doors before entering? I'd really like my privacy. Thanks for hearing me out.

28

A TIP

When talking with your parents, picture a sandwich. You start out with sweet, soft bread, which represents a kind, thoughtful comment. The statement in the middle is the "meat"—that is, exactly what you're asking for, the meat of the issue. Then you add another piece of soft bread to end on a positive note. That's it! And remember: A little humor can spice up any sandwich.

building your case

Whining, begging, and pestering your parents usually won't help you get what you want. Instead, learn the steps below to improve your chances—now and in the future.

1. **List the pros and cons** of the issue, including the facts and your feelings.

2. Imagine all the problems your parents might see, **find solutions** to those problems, and bring them with you.

3. Choose a **good time** and a **quiet place** to talk, and ask your parents to meet then to "hear you out."

4. **Present the list** to your parents.

5. Don't ask for a decision! Instead, **ask your parents to just think** about your request.

6. Ask your parents for **a specific time to check back** with them for an answer.

7. **Be patient** for that answer. Bugging your parents will only hurt your case.

Here's how it might work.

Is there something you've been wanting to ask for? Take a look at the example below on how you can build your case. Do you notice how it follows the steps shown on the left page?

Why giving me a bigger allowance is a good idea

PROS:

I'll be able to save for the MP3 player I want.

I won't bother my parents with asking for money all the time.

CONS:

My parents are already on a tight budget.

I'm not doing anything extra to earn more money.

PROBLEMS MY PARENTS MIGHT SEE:

They'll give me more money, but then I'll still ask them for

other stuff I want.

I'm not managing the allowance I have right now.

SOLUTIONS:

I promise to . . .

* not ask for money to spend on extras or treats

at the store.

* set some money aside for the more expensive things I want.

* do research on money management for kids.

* take on more responsibility, like feeding the dog before

and after school.

Signed _Macie_   Date _Aug. 4_

how to compromise

Remember in kindergarten when you learned your colors? You loved blue and your friend loved red, but when you colored them together, you made purple. Well, compromising is like that—you take two (or more) ideas and combine them to create a brand-new idea that everyone can agree on. Here's how you do it:

You to your parents:

I really want to stay up late.

Your parents:

We want to make sure you're getting enough sleep.

Compromise:
You and your parents decide that you can stay up later for one week, and then you'll revisit the issue after you all see how well the change worked.

You to your friend:

Hey, it's really nice outside. Let's get out and enjoy the sunshine after being inside all week.

Your friend:

But I love to play board games. Why can't we ever do what I like to do?

Compromise:
You and your friend agree to play board games on a blanket in the backyard.

You to your sister:

Just because we share a room doesn't mean you get to take it over. When my friends are here, I want privacy.

Your sister:

It's my room, too!

Compromise:
You and your sister agree that when you bring friends over, she'll stay out of the room until they leave, unless she's invited to stay. And you'll do the same when her friends come over.

You to your dad:

Dad, it upsets me that you want me to win every soccer match. I can't be perfect, so your criticism is ruining the fun for me.

Your dad:

I want you to give it your best and keep improving.

Compromise:
You promise to work hard and give the sport your best effort, but ask your dad to accept the results of the game—or at least not to discuss them with you for 24 hours.

You to your friend:

Samantha, I want to run around at recess and play with all my friends.

Your friend:

Well, I want more alone time to just talk with you.

Compromise:
You agree to spend more time with your friend after school, but you'll both play with your other friends at recess.

getting it right

Think you know the best way to ask for what you want? Test your knowledge by taking this quiz. Circle the answer that fits you best.

1. You want to go to a movie this weekend with a group of friends, but you haven't gone to a movie without a parent yet.

   a. "Mom, I know you're cooking dinner, but I need to ask: Can I go to the movies with my friends?"

   b. "Mom, is now a good time to talk with you about this weekend?"

2. You want to borrow your friend's favorite hat for a skit you're doing in class.

   a. "Can I borrow your hat for the play? I'll take good care of it and get it right back to you."

   b. "Hey, you know that hat you have? I need it."

3. Your little sister wants to borrow your socks for the hundredth time, and you're tired of it.

   a. "Mom! Can you help Fannie find her socks? She can't find hers and needs a pair."

   b. "Here's a pair, Fannie. But this means you have to agree to help me find your socks and pair them up after school."

4. You want your mom to stop picking out your clothes for you in the morning.

   a. "Mom, I'm not a little kid. I'm going to pick out my own clothes from now on."

   b. "You have great style, Mom, but I'm older now, and I think I should start picking out my own clothes. I still want to hear your advice, though."

5. You want to watch a TV show that the whole school is talking about, but it's on after your bedtime.

   a. "Mom and Dad, what if I record the show, or watch it online, or stay up and watch it with you to see if you think it's OK?"

   b. "Why can't I watch this show? All of my friends' parents let them stay up and watch it."

Answers

1. The answer is b. You know that **timing is important.** If you approach your mom when she's in the middle of something, you're less likely to get the results you want. If you're not sure when it's a good time to ask your question, ask your mom if she's free to talk.

2. The answer is a. **Reassuring your friend** that you understand the responsibility involved in borrowing her things will help her feel more comfortable loaning them to you. Now the key is to follow through with what you've promised.

3. The answer is b. Is it your job to find your little sister's socks? Probably not, but **offering a compromise** is the right thing to do. Not only are you pitching in, which is part of being in a family, but also you're helping yourself from being bothered for socks in the future.

4. The answer is b. You understand that **sandwiching your request** between two loving comments is a good way to ask for what you want without offending. Pass the mayo!

5. The answer is a. Every family has different rules. You're not always going to get what you want, but by **making your case in a respectful way,** you'll increase your chances and impress your parents along the way.

what other girls are saying about
how they get what they want

I always say 'excuse me' before asking for what I want. If I start out polite, it almost always works out.

It's hard not to beg my parents, but it usually just makes them mad. So I just say, 'I'll leave the room so I don't annoy you and let you think.'

I tell my parents how much the item means to me, and I ask if I can earn it. For example, 'Mom and Dad, can I please have a hamster? We haven't had a pet in so long, and I miss having one. What can I do to show you that I'm responsible enough to get one?'

if you need to say "no"

You can say no in a kind way without explaining or saying a whole lot more. If you have another solution, that's great, but if not, politely decline. Period.

If friends want necklaces like the one you made, but it would take too much time:

> I'm afraid that I don't have the time to make all these. I can teach you guys how to do it, though.

If a friend invites you over to her house, but you don't want to go:

> It's not going to work out today; sorry. But maybe another time?

If your friend's mom offers you a taste of a new recipe, but you don't like how it smells:

> No, but thanks anyway.

If your friend wants to take your new MP3 player home for the night, but you don't want to loan it out:

> I'm not comfortable with that, but do you want to listen to it in my room now?

If you're invited to a scary movie, but the thought terrifies you:

> Oh, I don't like those kinds of movies. I'd go see the one about the dog, though.

If your best friend asks you to try out for cheerleading with her, but you want to run for student council:

> Thanks for thinking of me! It's just not my thing.

If the girls in your class want to chase the boys at recess, but you have no interest:

> You guys go ahead.

If your coach asks if you can play in the tournament next weekend, but you have plans:

> Thanks for thinking of me, but my family will be out of town.

If your teacher asks you to be in a spelling bee, but your knees are knocking thinking about it:

> I don't think I'm quite ready, but thanks for asking!

BIG IMPORTANT POINT
It's OK to say no. Really, it is!

ways to say "no"

To avoid stumbling over your words when the moment to decline arrives, practice these creative options to "No, thanks."

No-can-do.

Not this time, thanks!

Until I check, let's assume I can't.

That won't work for me.

Absolutely not.

Try me again later.

Nah. Thanks, though!

I'm sorry, but I'm already busy then.

Sorry, but let me know how it goes.

I appreciate the thought, but I can't.

I need to sit that one out.

Uh-uh. Nothing personal, though.

I know my limits, so I gotta say no.

That doesn't suit my personality, I'm afraid.

making it right

Nobody's perfect. We *all* make mistakes. It's not just part of growing up, it's part of life. But just like when you make a mess, it's your job to clean it up. When you make a mistake, you've got to make it right.

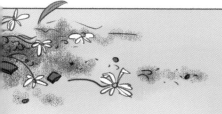

how to apologize for almost anything

Try the step-by-step apology below. It makes saying "I messed up" as easy as 1-2-3.

Step 1: Clearly admit what you did, and apologize.

Step 2: Explain why it was wrong and that you "get" it was wrong.

Step 3: If possible, offer to take action to correct the mistake.

Your apologies will look like this one.

1. Admit what you did and apologize.

2. Explain why it was wrong.

3. Offer to take action.

Now you try.

Think of a mistake that you've made recently. How can you make it right? Following the 1-2-3 steps, write your answer here:

BIG IMPORTANT POINT

Finding the courage to deliver an apology might not be easy, but do it anyway. The person you're apologizing to will appreciate that you're taking responsibility for your actions. And believe it or not, apologizing well is a sure sign of a confident person.

if you betray your friend

If you want a friend to continue to trust you, you need to let her know that you've made a mistake—and that you want to fix it. And you need to let her know before someone else does, or it'll seem that you just got caught making the blunder rather than sincerely being sorry.

If you tell your friend that you don't want to go to the movies, and then you and another friend bump into her at the theater:

> I didn't want to hurt your feelings. I'm sorry if I did. I should've been honest. Next time, I'll tell you the truth.

If you promise your friend that you'll come over, but you don't show up at her house:

> Breaking my promise to you was not OK. And not calling you was rude. I made some really stupid choices today, and I'm sorry. I won't ever do this again.

If you make up a big lie about your friend and she finds out:

> I was trying to be a big shot. I understand that you're mad at me, but I want to make this right. I'll tell the others I lied, and I promise I'll never do anything like this again. I am so sorry.

If your friend tells you something about another girl, and then you run right over and tell that girl what your friend said:

> I made a huge mistake. You trusted me, and I let you down. I promise that if you trust me again, I'll keep my big mouth shut.

Keep this in mind.

• Don't avoid an apology. Time alone won't heal things.

• A fake apology is worse than no apology. Speak from the heart, or you'll only make things worse.

• Admitting you made a mistake doesn't make you weak. In fact, you'll appear more confident if you are able to face your flaws and work to fix the situation.

• If you promise not to do it again—don't. Repeat offenses make you an unsupportive, unreliable, and unsatisfying friend. And who would want a friend like that?

if you hurt someone on purpose

Hurting someone on purpose is one of the worst mistakes you can make. If you hurt another person with your words or actions—whether you're caught or not—the pain you've caused will last until you can make it right.

If you're upset and jealous of a friend, so you spread a rumor about her mom:

> I started the rumor. It was wrong, and I realize this has probably cost me your friendship. I'll do my best to let everyone know it's not true. I really am sorry.

If you receive an e-mail about a boy in your class, and instead of deleting it, you send it to everyone in your address book:

> (To the boy)
> I'm ashamed that I didn't delete the e-mail when I got it. I'm sorry, and I'll try to put a stop to it.

> (To friends)
> Guys, that e-mail is cyberbullying. Please delete it.

If kids say mean things to a girl on the bus, and you laugh right along, but when you see her, she won't speak to you:

I know I hurt your feelings today, Maria. I'm sorry. I should've stood up for you. Can you forgive me?

If kids ask if you're related to your "nerdy" brother, and you say "No," and then he asks you if it's true you lied:

I didn't know what to say, John. I blurted out "No," but I didn't mean it. I love you, and I'm glad that you're my brother. You're far more important to me than what they think.

BIG IMPORTANT POINT

If you hurt someone on purpose, sincerely ask for forgiveness. And then brace yourself. You might not be instantly forgiven. It's important that you respect the other person's feelings, and that means being patient— for as long as it takes.

49

if you upset your teacher

No one wants teacher trouble. Whether you're breaking a rule or not doing your best, disappointing a teacher feels awful. If you know that you've crossed a line, it's important to work it out as soon as possible.

If your friend copies your book report and your teacher finds out:

I should not have shared my work. I was trying to help a friend, but this wasn't the way, and it won't ever happen again.

If your teacher blames someone else for something you did:

Mr. Jay, I need to talk with you. Aubrey didn't write that note about Mia—I did. I'm sorry, and I'll apologize to Mia right away.

If your piano teacher is frustrated because you haven't been practicing:

> I need to work on this more. I'll make sure I get my practice time in this week. I'm sorry I wasn't prepared. I don't want to waste your time—or mine.

If your teacher catches you talking about something really offensive and changes her attitude toward you:

> I think I offended you today. I understand that was really inappropriate, and I'm sorry. I feel bad about it, and it won't happen again.

Tips about teachers

1. Timing is important. Look for a time when your teacher isn't being pulled in ten directions, or ask to set up a private time with her or him.

2. Be respectful. Be respectful. Be respectful. If you're not, your message will be lost.

3. If you continue to run into problems communicating with your teacher, reach out for help from a parent, a school guidance counselor, or a principal.

BIG IMPORTANT POINT
Teachers were young once, too, and they've made their share of mistakes. Just make sure you let them know that you're learning from yours.

if you forget
something important

If your memory fails you, the first thing you need to do is apologize. And then quickly create a plan to make it right. Check out these examples below.

If your best friend's parents recently divorced, and your friend has to keep reminding you that her mom's last name is now different from her last name:

Instead of this: "How am I supposed to remember?"

Say this:

> Jill, I'm sorry I keep forgetting. (Repeat her mom's name out loud three times.) Wilson, Wilson, Wilson. Next time I'll get it right.

If you borrow something and forget to bring it back to school:

Instead of this: "Yeah, I don't know where your book is. Anyway, it's no big deal. I'll get it to you soon."

Say this:

> I'm sorry, Ms. Hill, but I forgot your book today. I could call my parents or write myself a note to bring it in tomorrow. Which would you prefer?

If it's your friend's birthday and you forget:

Instead of this: "Uh, I knew you had a birthday, but a family emergency came up."

Say this: Happy belated birthday! I'm so sorry I forgot your party. I hope you had a wonderful day. Let's have our own make-up celebration this Saturday.

If your mom asks you to be home for dinner, but you forget, and she has to track you down at a neighbor's house:

Instead of this: "Why didn't you call and remind me? You know I don't wear a watch."

Say this: I'm so sorry! I totally lost track of time. I should have asked Mrs. Currin for a reminder. Can I bring the food to the table?

what other girls are saying about
forgetting

If I forget the words to something, I just make up others that still make sense.

My parents leave me notes to help me remember.

I forgot to bring my violin to school on the day I had a lesson. I looked at my teacher and said, 'I blew it. I have no excuse. I just forgot. I'm really sorry.' She just said, 'Mistakes happen.'

Once I tried to introduce my friend, and I forgot her name! I just said, 'I'm having a mental block! Sorry!' She rescued me, and we all laughed about it.

If I forget something, I just say, 'I'm so embarrassed!' And I am!

When I forget what I'm about to say, I just say, 'Hold on. Now where was I?'

Forgetting happens to me all the time. I say, 'Oh, duh. I just forgot what I was going to say.' Then the person with me usually reminds me.

If I'm afraid I'll forget something I need at school, I call and leave myself a message on the answering machine at home!

I forget a lot, so I ask my parents to help me remember.

that hurts

We all react differently when our feelings are hurt—some of us yell, some of us run and hide, and some of us burst out crying. These strong emotions need attention. But saying the wrong thing could make the situation worse. When our feelings are hurt, it's best to step back, think the situation through, and then decide the next, best step.

anger inventory

What do you do when you're fuming mad? Fill out the worksheet below to find out.

I get angry when I see this happening:

I get angry when I hear about this happening:

I get angry when my parents tell me about this:

The things you've listed above are your "hot buttons."
A hot button is something that causes you to react emotionally.

Sometimes a sibling will say this just to make me angry:

Sometimes a friend or schoolmate will say this just to make me angry:

When people say the things you've listed above, they're "pushing your buttons." That means that people can say certain words (or do certain things) to _intentionally_ make you angry.

When I'm angry, I usually:

This is how you've dealt with your anger in the past. But now that you know what your "buttons" are, you can try to recover from your anger more quickly. Read the **Big Truths about Anger** below, and then write down a better way to deal with your anger.

BIG TRUTHS ABOUT ANGER

- Anger is a normal, natural feeling.

- Your body might warn you when you're getting angry with a faster heartbeat, increased breathing, and clenched teeth.

- When you're angry, it's difficult to think clearly. It helps to step back, breathe deeply, and think about your options.

- It's absolutely possible to be angry and still stay in control.

- When you're angry, it's better to say nothing (at first) than to say the wrong thing. Once you've cooled down, you can decide what to do next.

- Writing your angry thoughts down (and then ripping them up) is a great way to get your feelings out BEFORE talking to the person who has upset you.

When my buttons are pushed, I will try to:

this makes me mad!

If a friend intentionally tries to hurt your feelings or make you angry, you need to respond to her. If you don't, you might feel stomped on and resent her, which will hurt your friendship. Practice using the responses below.

COLD AS ICE
Your friend tries to get her way by giving you the silent treatment.

Step away. If you give in to your friend's game, she'll keep using it as a tactic to manipulate you.

You say:

> If you want to talk to me about something, I'll listen, but this feels like a game, and I'm not playing.

INSULTER
Your friend often says mean things to you and then covers it up with "JK" (just kidding). Now she's about to do it again.

See it coming. You've heard this put-down before, so stop it in its tracks.

You say:

> Hold on. I feel an insult coming, and I'm pretty sure I don't want to hear it.

LOOSE LIPPED

You tell your friend something in private, she texts it to a friend, and now everyone knows.

Call her out. Let your friend know that what she did wasn't cool.

You say:

> I wouldn't have done that to you.
> I'm mad right now.

FAKE FRIEND

Your "friend" draws attention to every slip, trip, popped button, and other embarrassing incident you go through.

Act confused. With a curious reply, you'll put the ball back in her court.

You say:

> Seriously? Why would you do that?

ONE-UPPER

Your friend keeps asking you about your things as a way to brag about her things.

Be a broken record. Don't give in just because a friend keeps asking. Repeat the same answer again and again.

You say:

> You keep asking and I keep telling you that "things" don't mean that much to me. Let's change the subject.

BIG IMPORTANT POINT

When someone tries to make you look bad, it's a warning sign. This isn't how friendship is supposed to feel. Be careful, and don't be afraid to pull away from friends who make you feel bad about yourself.

if a friend lets you down

Most of the time friendships should be easy, but for those times when the road gets rocky, remember this: Friends should have an equal balance of power. The thoughts, wishes, and opinions of each of you should matter.

If a friend tells you who to sit by at lunch, who to play with at recess, and who to invite over after school:

> Hey, Lysa. Thanks for the input, but I need to make my own decisions.

If your classmates are chatting loudly about a slumber party, but you're not invited:

> Really, guys? This is seriously hurtful. Can you stop, please?

If your friend takes something you've said the wrong way, and she starts shouting at you:

> Hold on! I didn't mean it THAT way. Please hear me out.

If you and your best friend have *another* argument, and now you want to tell her that the two of you might need to take a break:

> Maddie, we've been fighting way too much lately. I think we should take a break for a week and talk after that.

If a friend demands to know if she's your best friend:

Please don't pressure me. We're friends. Let's leave it at that.

If a friend asks what your favorite movie is, and then she makes fun of your answer:

Hey, I didn't make fun of your answer. Let's change the subject.

If, at the lunch table, girls are talking about a TV show, and a friend tells everyone that you're not allowed to watch it:

It's no big deal to me, though. We just don't watch that one at my house.

A TIP

When you and a friend are trying to solve a problem, say what's on *your* mind. Don't try to second-guess what your friend might be feeling or thinking. That's for her to tell you. If you really, truly listen to each other, you'll find a solution to your problem more quickly.

if someone is being teased

If you see someone being teased who isn't standing up for herself, you need to step in and help. Change the subject, add some humor, or offer reassurance.

If kids are teasing someone who has special needs:

> Knock it off. That's so wrong.

If students are teasing a kid about an incident that happened last year:

> Come on, that's ancient history. Turn the page!

If girls are teasing a friend because she gets her period and isn't prepared:

> Leave her alone. It might be you someday, and you wouldn't want us to tease you.

If a quiet boy in your class throws up and classmates make fun of him, and then the teacher asks you to walk him to the office:

> Don't feel bad. It could happen to anyone. It's not a big deal. Really.

BIG IMPORTANT POINT
If teasing continues, it's called harassment, and it needs to be reported. It's the right thing to do.

if you're being teased

Teasing is meant to embarrass you, but don't let anyone shake your confidence. Instead, come back with words that help you sound cool, calm, and collected.

If classmates tease you about a boy who's just a friend:

> Just wait, and one day you'll see. Girls and boys can be friends—it's true!

If your favorite relative teases you about having a boyfriend:

> I don't have a boyfriend yet, Uncle Josh. I'm only in the fifth grade.

If people make fun of your glasses:

> Yeah, yeah. Call me four eyes. I can take it.

A TIP
Move through the initial embarrassment of teasing, and come back sure and strong—but remember that if the teasing doesn't stop, you need to involve an adult.

dealing with bullies

To see how well you stand up for yourself, circle each answer that best fits the reply you'd give to a bully.

1. A girl in your class tells you that she wishes you weren't seated next to her. You say . . .

a. Why? What's wrong with me?

b. You're not exactly my first choice either.

c. I can't believe you just said that.

2. You're running for class president, and a classmate says he would never vote for a redhead. You say . . .

a. That is so mean.

b. I couldn't care less. I don't need your stupid vote.

c. Why on earth would you say that to me?

3. The queen bee informs you at lunch that you're not invited to play at recess. You say . . .

a. Are you mad at me? What did I do wrong? Why?

b. I don't want to play your dumb baby games anyway. Grow up!

c. Really? Hmmm . . . interesting.

4. Your "friend" Teena tells you that if you hang out with anyone but her outside of school, your friendship is over. You say . . .

a. Can I at least play with my neighbors?

b. No one is the boss of me. Shut up!

c. That will never work. I'm surprised you'd even suggest it.

5. A girl comes up to you in gym class and says, "No one here likes you." You say . . .

a. (Nothing. You burst into tears and head to the office to call home.)

b. Who'd want to be friends with you, anyway?

c. I'm shocked you'd even say that to me. I didn't think you were that kind of a person.

6. Your classmate says with a smirk, "You're so pretty!" when she obviously means the opposite. You say . . .

a. Thanks. (Then you put your head down and feel like a complete laughingstock as she giggles and walks away.)

b. I know what you mean. I won't fall for it!

c. Really? And you are so nice to say that!

Answers

Mostly a's
It's better to say almost anything (or walk away) than to beg for someone's approval. No one can push you around unless you let them. So don't let them. Ever.

Mostly b's
It's one thing to stand up for yourself, but quite another to BECOME a bully or a jerk in the process. Even though it's sometimes tempting, don't allow yourself to mirror the mean person looking you in the face.

Mostly c's
Acting surprised is a great technique to deal with cruelty. Don't even react to or acknowledge the mean comment. Instead, react to the fact that the person saying it is being mean. Then speak up in a way that isn't mean. Being surprised will make the bully reconsider her behavior, which is exactly the point.

staying strong around mean kids

Bullies like to challenge your confidence. They defy you to remember who you are. They dare you to find the right words to reply to them. And they lure you into becoming one of them in the process. So how do you say what you mean without being mean?

Practice.

Practice.

Practice.

Finding the right words to say is the easy part, but using them while someone is trying to hurt you is another. You need to practice the words until they feel natural. Say your words in front of a mirror, in the shower, with your parents or big sister, or under your covers. Be prepared for that time when a mean kid is in your face.

Practice **the four W's** below. One of them is likely to work in most situations.

Raise an eyebrow when you say this, as if to mean, "You've got problems" or "I can't believe you just said that." It'll make the person second-guess herself and maybe even make her feel ashamed.

Look confused when you say this, as if to mean, "I didn't hear you" or "I have no clue what you're saying." Either way, the person will have to repeat herself, and no one likes to do that.

Look surprised, as if to say, "Yikes, get a hold of yourself" or "You've stepped over the line." Most often this is embarrassing enough to shut a person down.

Show your very best bored look, as if you couldn't care less what the person's saying. It lets her know that she can't have your power.

BIG IMPORTANT POINT
Many times, one word is enough to stop a mean kid in her tracks. No one deserves to be bullied. If it continues for more than a few days, report it to an adult you trust. The sooner a bully is shut down, the better.

clever comebacks

When dealing with a bully, you don't want to be aggressive, but you don't want to be a pushover, either. Find a few words on the list that fit your personality, and use them.

- Really? Seriously?

- Oh, please.

- That's just wrong.

- (Shaking head) Dude.

- Rightbackatcha!

- Having a bad day?

- Oooo-Kaaay.

- Happy now?

- So rude.

- That's impressive—not.

- Are you done?

- That's some negative energy you got.

- What's your deal?

- That's your opinion.

- FYI: It's a free country.

- Not cool.

- (Point to ear) I can't hear you.

- There's no nice way to respond, so I won't.

- Yes! That's what I was hoping for.

- And you have a great day!

- There should be a rule against that.

- Is this an attempt at humor?

- You're allowed to have an opinion.

- I can't tell you how little I care.

- Not listening . . .

- Oh, yeah, right, uh-huh, OK, yep.

- Whatever floats your boat.

- Have you ever heard of karma?

- There's help for that.

- That's your problem, not mine.

- Oh, you're trying to be clever!

- Excuse me?

- That means absolutely nothing.

- I really had no idea.

- Feel better?

- Don't talk to me.

- So?

- I have no idea what you mean.

- Stress much?

- Thanks for sharing!

71

dealing with difficult adults

When an adult hurts your feelings, it's tough to know how to react. You want to lash out, but that could get you into trouble. The best reaction is to be calm and confident while still being respectful.

Start with "I," not "you." Don't tell others how they feel—state how you feel.

> Look at this sloppy paper. It looks like you don't even care about your work!

> I don't have the best handwriting, and I may have rushed through this, but I do care. I'll try to be neater next time.

Consider another point of view before offering yours.

> I'm sorry, but I don't think a young lady should be outside playing football.

> That's something to think about. But I believe . . .

Avoid "always" and "never." For example, "You always blame me!" or "You never yell at the others." These words can anger adults. Instead, focus on the question, not the emotion.

Stay calm, don't interrupt, and stick to the facts.

Now you try it.
Think of a situation where an adult upset you. How could you have responded to that person in a way that was respectful but also helped make the situation better for you?

73

sad times

Sad times happen in life. They just do. But you can help friends and family through their sadness by being there. "Being there" can mean different things. Sometimes it's offering a plate of cookies or a hug. Sometimes it's taking the person's mind off of her sadness or listening while she pours her heart out. What's most important is that you follow her lead and offer comfort when you can.

if your friend's pet dies

When a friend's pet dies, it's absolutely OK to try to help by asking her how she's doing. Just be sure that your voice isn't filled with pity, which might embarrass your friend. Keep your comments brief, and then listen for her response. Trust that if your friend wants to talk more about it, she'll let you know.

If your friend's pet dies, and you're afraid to ask her about it:

> I know you're sad about Blossom, but if you want to talk, I'm here.

If a car hits a friend's dog that you knew and loved:

> I'm so sorry about Buttons. I loved taking him on walks with you. Remember that time a butterfly landed on his nose and he just stared at it? We laughed until my belly hurt.

If the cat your friend adores runs away from home, and your friend is afraid she's gone forever:

> I'm sorry you're going through this. Do you want to create some 'lost cat' posters?

If your friend's family made the difficult decision to put their sick dog to sleep:

> I know you didn't want Emma to suffer anymore, but I imagine it's still really hard. Do you want to talk about it?

A TIP
If a friend's pet dies, don't ramble on about your pets. Listen, and keep the focus on your friend.

if your pet dies

Saying good-bye when a pet dies can be heartbreaking. Check out these examples.

If you need to tell your friends that your beloved dog was put to sleep:

> I had a really tough weekend, and I'm still very upset. We had to put my dog Champ to sleep. It was the hardest thing ever, so I'm not in a great mood.

If you're afraid you'll start crying when people ask about your pet dying:

> (Say quickly) It's been tough. Thanks for asking.

If a friend tells you that you can always just get another pet:

> I wish it were that easy. I know you mean well, but I'm just really feeling sad today.

If you tell a friend your dog died, and she doesn't say anything but then talks about an amusement park she wants to go see:

> Hey, I'm not feeling that well today. I'll talk to you later. Bye.

when someone you know is sick

When you visit a person who's sick or injured, bring a confident attitude with you to help that person find the confidence she needs to deal with her situation. While visiting, try to imagine yourself in her place. What would you want her to say to you? And if you get stuck, don't worry. Just being there will mean a lot.

If you're visiting your sick grandpa in the hospital, and you're not sure what to say to him:

(When you see your grandpa, squeeze his hand and lovingly look into his eyes.) Hi, Grandpa! I brought you the comics because I know you like them.

If your best friend tells you that she's really scared because her mother has breast cancer:

Annie, your mom is a strong person. And now that the doctors know what she has, they can start helping her heal. We could make your mom some cards or posters to keep her spirits up.

If a boy with a heart condition has been gone from school for weeks, and he returns to class:

Welcome back, Jonah! I'm glad you're feeling better. Everyone's missed you so much.

If your neighbor is finally home after a car accident, and you want to do something nice for her:

I'm sorry to hear about the accident. My family has been thinking about you, so we made you some muffins.

If your sister finds out she has asthma, and she's really scared:

I'm sorry, Lily. I know you're kind of scared, but I'm going to help you work this out. You and I can get through anything together.

If your father has to have a surgery, and you're nervous:

Dad, I'm really scared that you're going into the hospital. Can we talk about it?

A TIP

Visiting someone who's sick can be awkward and sometimes scary, especially if the person is in the hospital. Try to relax and be yourself. A pleasant visit with you will really brighten a sick person's day.

reaching out

You're visiting someone who's recovering from an illness—and you don't know what to say! Try these silly questions to bring cheer to someone dear.

Jot down *your* answer to each question below, and then ask your friend the question. As you go along, discuss each response to discover why your choices matched—or didn't!

Would you rather . . .

1. know how to speak to animals, how to speak to plants, or how to speak every language on the planet?

My answer:

My friend's answer:

2. spend one day each week at a slumber party, at the movies, or at a new restaurant?

My answer:

My friend's answer:

3. speak every word out of your mouth like a parrot, like a robot, or like a movie announcer? (Try it!)

My answer:

My friend's answer:

4. spend six months living in a giant goldfish bowl, in a mountain cave, or in an igloo?

My answer:

My friend's answer:

5. be the world's funniest girl, strongest girl, or smartest girl?

My answer:

My friend's answer:

6. eat pizza, eat peanut-butter sandwiches, or eat grilled cheese every day for one month?

My answer:

My friend's answer:

7. live the rest of your life without music, without TV and movies, or without books?

My answer:

My friend's answer:

8. spend an entire day breathing underwater, being invisible, or flying?

My answer:

My friend's answer:

9. walk around with a monkey's tail, an elephant's ears, or a giraffe's neck?

My answer:

My friend's answer:

10. spend a night alone in a zoo, in a museum, or in a library?

My answer:

My friend's answer:

if your friend is moving away

If you're faced with a close friend moving away, don't agonize—organize! Get creative and find ways to let your friend know how much she means to you.

Your friend told you she's moving, and now she's avoiding you:

> Can we talk? I feel like you're blowing me off, and it really hurts. Just because you're moving doesn't mean our friendship needs to end. Want to hear my plans?

If your friend breaks the news that she's moving at the end of the school year:

> I'll miss you so much, but I'm your friend now, and I always will be.

If your friend's parent is out of work, so her family is being forced to move:

> I'm sure your parents have a plan and are doing what they feel is best. Still, I know it's hard, so I'm here if you want to vent.

if you're moving away

If you've just found out that you're moving, you might be dealing with lots of different emotions. Just remember that while change is difficult, it's also temporary. At some point, life will feel normal again—really it will.

If you told your friend that you're moving, and she acts as if she doesn't care:

We need to talk about the move. You haven't said anything about it since I told you, and I could really use some support.

If you're terrified to tell your best friend since kindergarten that you are moving halfway across the country:

I've been meaning to talk with you. I have some bad news, and I don't want you to hear it from anyone else but me.

If you're thrilled to be moving closer to your dad, but your friend isn't happy for you:

Don't get me wrong. I'm sad to move away from you, but I really miss my dad. I hope you understand.

If you've accepted the fact that you have to move, but your older sister has been crying for days:

I know you'll miss your friends, but you're a great person, and kids in the new school will see that. In the meantime, you've always got me.

if your friend's parents divorce

When parents separate, kids face a storm of feelings. For some girls, it might feel like a welcome relief from the tension at home. But for many, it'll feel downright devastating. So if a friend's parents divorce, be sensitive to her feelings and accept them, whatever they are.

If your best friend's parents divorce, and she tries to act happy, but you know she's hiding the fact that she's miserable:

I'm sorry to hear about your parents. Let me know what I can do to help. I'll be here to listen if you want to share.

If your cousin calls, crying hysterically, because she just found out her parents are separating:

I know you're upset, Tammie, and I can only imagine how you must feel right now.
(Then be quiet, and let your cousin talk.)

If your friend's parents are divorcing, and you feel worse about it than your friend does (or acts like she does):

Wow, I admire your positive attitude. Just know that if you have a bad day, I'm here.

if your parents divorce

If your family is changing, be gentle with yourself. That means take the time to be sad, but also let yourself be happy and excited at the new beginnings. Remember, even after a divorce, your family is still *your family*—and always will be.

If your parents tell you that they're separating, and they want to know what you're feeling:

> I don't know what to say. I'm having all sorts of feelings. It might take some time to sort them out.

If you haven't slept in days because you're really hurting about your parents' divorce, and you think you need help dealing with it:

> Mom, I know things are tough right now, but I think I need to talk to someone about you and Dad divorcing. Do you have any suggestions?

You've been avoiding the subject for months, but now you need to tell your best friend about your parents' divorce:

> Hey, I'd like to talk to you about something really personal. My mom and dad are getting a divorce. It's been very tough on me, so I'm hoping that you can help me get through it.

If a friend's mom asks where your dad has been lately—and you freeze because he no longer lives at home:

> My family is changing—maybe you could talk to my mom about it.

if someone in your friend's family dies

If your friend is hurting, it's better to chance sounding awkward than to pretend nothing's wrong. Be brave. Speak from your heart, and be the best friend you can. You won't regret it.

If your best friend's dad dies:

> I am so sorry about your dad. If you want to talk, I'll listen.

If a friend misses school for her great-grandma's funeral, and it's her first day back:

> I'm sorry to hear about your great-grandma. I'll be glad to help you get caught up with anything.

If tragedy strikes your friend's family, and your friend looks stressed:

> I'm here if you want to talk, but if you just want to play a game of cards and NOT talk about what happened, we can do that, too.

If your friend's brother died a week ago, and now you're not sure if you can say his name out loud or even mention him:

> I want you to know that if you ever want to talk about your brother, it's OK. I'll listen.

A TIP

After someone a friend knows has died, respect that the situation is sad. Your friend may not be happy for a while, and that's OK.

if someone in your family dies

Dealing with a loved one's death is one of the most difficult things we go through in life. Talk or write about your feelings, and if you have questions, ask an adult. You don't have to go through this alone.

If your grandpa dies, and you don't know what to say when people ask you how you're doing, because you're not doing very well:

I'm sad about Grandpa, and I'm worried about Dad, too. It's been really hard on all of us.

If someone in your family dies, and people keep coming up to you at the funeral to say how sorry they are:

Thanks. That means a lot.

If you want to comfort your mom after your grandma dies, but you're really upset, too:

(You don't have to say a thing. Sit quietly with your mom. Hold each other, and let the tears come.)

supporting a grieving person

To help a friend who is grieving, imagine that you're going through what she's going through. Which of the comments below would help you and which wouldn't? Circle your answers.

1. "You're in my thoughts and prayers."
   Helpful   Not helpful

2. "At least she's in a better place now."
   Helpful   Not helpful

3. "I'm so sorry."
   Helpful   Not helpful

4. "Try not to think about it."
   Helpful   Not helpful

5. "Things happen for a reason."
   Helpful   Not helpful

6. "I'm here if you need me."
   Helpful   Not helpful

7. "I remember when I first met your brother. We were at your house and . . ."
   Helpful   Not helpful

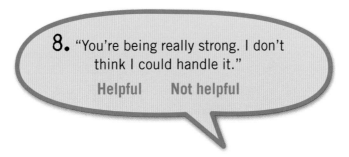

8. "You're being really strong. I don't think I could handle it."

Helpful   Not helpful

Answers

1. Helpful
   You'll likely hear this comment many times in life. It says, "I'll think of you in the days to come" and recognizes how hard those days might be.

2. Not helpful
   People have different beliefs. And when a person is missing someone who has died, it's hard to look at any bright side.

3. Helpful
   This says, "I'm sorry that you have to go through such a painful experience. I wish you didn't."

4. Not helpful
   This is more about you. It says, "I can't stand to see you like this, so stop it." But people need to grieve, so allow it to happen.

5. Not helpful
   Death is confusing enough. Imagining the loss was for a particular reason is not very comforting.

6. Helpful
   This says, "Whatever you need, I'm here to help." And even if there's nothing you can do to ease that person's pain, knowing you would if you could will mean a lot.

7. Helpful
   Sharing memories of the person who died says that you respected him and that you're willing to talk about (and listen to) all the wonderful things about him.

8. Not helpful
   Even though this is meant to be a compliment, you never want the grieving person to feel she has to pretend to be OK around you. Sometimes she might appear really strong, but a meltdown might be right around the corner (and that's not a bad thing). Also, remember that this person has no choice but to deal with the loss—be sensitive to that.

I'm embarrassed!

Eventually, you'll do something embarrassing—everybody does. You'll trip, drop something, or say the wrong thing. If you draw attention to the mistake, people will notice (when probably no one would have noticed before!). So don't make a big deal about your mistake, and most likely others won't either.

about your family

Every family has its share of quirks and embarrassing moments. Use humor and grace to send a message that says, "Love me—love my family!" After all, friends come and go, but family is forever.

If you cringe every time your dad tells your friends his goofy jokes:	That's my dad. He's a funny one!
If your mom belts out the wrong lyrics on the radio with your friends in the car:	Parents—can't take 'em anywhere.
If your sister and her friends sing the dinosaur song to you in the halls, because you loved it as a little girl:	Oh, thanks! You're so sweet! I love that song.
If your dad chaperones your school dance and calls you "his little girl":	He'll still be saying that when I'm 30.
If your friend is over and your parents are disagreeing about some money issue—again:	Guess it's not a good day for grown-ups. They'll figure it out. How about we go play a game outside?

If you're embarrassed by your brother's silly behavior when friends are over:

He's a handful! Drives me crazy sometimes, but what can you do?

If your dad comes out in his neon Hawaiian shirt to take you and your friends skating:

Oh, Dad. Some things are better kept in the family, and I think that shirt is one of them. How attached are you to wearing it tonight?

If your mom snaps at your friends to "Go to sleep!" at your birthday party sleepover:

She's really tired and stressed. This party was a lot to put together. So let's settle down. See you in the A.M.

If your little sister annoys you by following you and your friends around EVERYWHERE—but your friends think she's cute:

She is cute—and fun, too. But if you want privacy, I'll ask my mom for help.

when you freeze up

Read the following situations. Do any of them sound familiar to you?

- A bossy girl asks you a question, but you can't think of a single word to say.

- You call your friend, and when the answering machine asks you to leave a message, you stutter out a non-answer.

- You can never greet people first in the halls.

- You decide not to buy a purse in a thrift store, because when you open your mouth to ask the clerk the price, nothing comes out.

- Your teacher calls on you, and even though your brain knows the answer, your mouth won't say it.

When these moments happen to you, it's likely that your brain is flooding with anxious energy. Here's what to do:

1. First, **BREATHE!** Deep breaths tell the brain that you're not under stress, and that makes it easier for you to think.

2. **MOVE YOUR BODY.** Shake off tension by moving your arms or legs.

3. **SAY ANYTHING.** Here are some suggestions:
   "Uh . . . "
   "Just a minute . . ."
   "I'm thinking . . ."
   "Hold on . . ."
   "I forgot what I was going to say . . ."

Practice these a lot with a parent or in the mirror. The more you repeat a response, the easier it'll be to pull out of your memory later.

4. **MOVE YOUR MOUTH.** Chew gum, drink water, or move your chin back and forth to help relax your facial muscles and jaws.

5. Keep breathing, and **KEEP TRYING.** If you find your tension getting worse, ask your doctor for more suggestions.

about your differences

You hide in the closet during thunderstorms, but your friend likes to listen to storms while going to sleep. You eat anything, but your friend eats only the same five foods. Fact is, our differences make us unique. So don't make a big deal about yours, and it's most likely that others won't either.

If a friend invites you to a sleepover, and you're afraid to sleep away from home:

> Oh, I'm not good at spending the night away from home. How about a half sleepover? I can go home at 10 or 11?

If your friend's mom serves a food that you won't eat, and she's curious why you didn't touch it:

> I filled up on the mashed potatoes. They were great!

If your friends ask you to join them in line at an amusement park ride, but you're afraid:

> I'm going to wait with the moms. This ride freaks me out.

If your family doesn't celebrate Christmas, and friends ask why:

> We're Jewish. We celebrate Hanukkah.

If your friend is showing a scary movie at her sleepover, but you know that you won't sleep after watching it:

There's no way I'm watching this. I'll just grab my book and headphones.

If your friend invites you to a boy/girl pool party, but you feel uncomfortable in a bathing suit around the boys:

I'd love to come, but I'm not sure I want to swim. Is that a problem?

If your Polish parents speak Polish around the house, and your friends ask why:

It's more comfortable for them. I can teach you a few words, if you like!

BIG IMPORTANT POINT
If everyone were the same, the world would be a very boring place.

it's personal

You might be a little on the nosy side if people are often surprised by your questions. To keep from offending people, make general statements, and let others decide how much they want to share. Check out our polite ways to satisfy your curiosity.

You can't believe how big your friend's house is.

Instead of this: "Look at this house. Are you rich?"

Say this:
> Don't you feel lucky to live in such a beautiful home?

Your friend has a very fancy coat that you love.

Instead of this: "Wow! How much did *that* coat cost?"

Say this:
> That is a fabulous coat!

You're curious about your friend's operation.

Instead of this: "When they took out your appendix, were your guts showing?"

Say this:
> So, tell me about your surgery.
> (Let your friend decide what she wants to share.)

If people ask **you** a nosy question, you can say politely but firmly, "I don't share that information." Another approach is to be as unclear as possible.

A cousin asks your weight.

Instead of this: "I, um, well, I weigh more than you."

Say this:

I don't keep track. I just try to be healthy.

A friend asks how much money your parents make.

Instead of this: "A lot!"

Say this: I don't know.

A classmate sees you taking medications and asks why.

Instead of this: "People's medical issues are private!"

Say this:
Oh, it's no big deal. I'm OK. Thanks for asking.
(If you're comfortable saying more, that's fine, but don't feel obligated.)

at a friend's awkward moment

Awkward moments happen. If a friend makes a mistake, help her feel comfortable enough to move on from it. Knowing what to say at delicate times will keep you at the top of everyone's list.

If your friend sleeps over and wets the bed:

It's not a big deal. Don't give it another thought.
(And then keep your lip zipped.)

If your teacher has a piece of food stuck in her teeth:

Ms. Seth, you might want to check in the mirror.
(Then gesture at your tooth with your finger.)

If your friend's zipper is down at the choral concert:

(Whisper) Shea . . . your zipper.

If your little sister has a runny nose:

Sissy, you need a tissue.

If your mom has bad breath and you want to tell her without embarrassing her:

(Whisper) Psst! Mom, you might need a mint or something.

at your awkward moment

If you feel embarrassed because of an accident or event, remember that what happened was awkward—not tragic. Really, if you act like IT'S NO BIG DEAL, it won't be.

If YOUR zipper is down, and your friend lets you know:

(Be calm, look away, and zip it up!)

If you drop your lunch tray in the crowded cafeteria:

(Smiling) I wasn't that hungry anyway.

If you trip over a ball in gym class and end up on your behind:

I'm cool. Yeah, that was graceful.

If you have friends over and your brother walks by the door in his underwear:

(Giggling) OK, so that was awkward!

saying the right thing

Words are powerful—once you say them, you can't easily take them back. Is there a way to communicate honestly without being hurtful? You bet.

to avoid hurting someone's feelings

You can't (and shouldn't) always give people the answers they want to hear, but making them feel bad is just wrong. Approach sensitive moments with grace and understanding. You'll be glad you did.

If a nice girl asks you to sit by her at lunch, but you'd rather stick with your best buds:

> Thanks for thinking of me. I'm going to stay where I am, but I appreciate the offer. Hey, would you like to join us?

If a boy you don't like asks you to dance, but you don't want to:

> I don't think so, but thank you anyway.

If a girl in class asks you to be her reading partner, but you'd rather buddy up with a friend:

> I usually pair up with Inga, so I feel like I should check with her first. Otherwise, I'd love to. Thanks for asking!

If your friend's house is oddly decorated and messy, but she wants to know what you think about her home:

> Your room is such a fun color, and I would love to have a Ping-Pong table in our living room.

If you don't think your friend draws very well, but she asks you what you think of her art:

> I like that you draw cats. I love cats!

If a friend asks you if you think the band she likes is better than the band another friend likes:

> I believe that the kind of music you like is a personal choice, so that's all I'm going to say about that.

If a friend asks you to be her best friend and gives you half of a best-friend necklace:

> Rather than one best friend, I like lots of close friends because there's less pressure. But you are one of my closest friends.

BIG IMPORTANT POINT

Letting someone down without hurting her feelings is all in your approach. If you're honest, kind, and respectful, she'll probably understand and accept your answer.

if someone takes advantage of you

If you feel someone your age is trying to take advantage of you, it may be tempting to ask a parent to come to your rescue. Instead, try handling the situation on your own first.

If a friend "borrows" a favorite shirt and never returns it:

> Hey, Vanessa! I need my shirt tomorrow. Do you want me to call you tonight and remind you?

If you tell your friend about an idea you have for a class project, and she steals the idea and presents it before you do:

> Erin, that was my idea! Taking it and using it was not cool.

If your desk partner has trouble understanding the teacher and always asks you to explain things to her:

> I need to get my work done. You should ask the teacher. Want me to get her for you?

If you work late to finish your homework, and then your friend calls at the last minute for your answers:

> That's cheating, Bridgette. I'm not doing that.

If you play a board game with a friend, and you catch her cheating:

> Whose set of rules are we playing with here?

If a friend borrows your cell phone every day and uses up a lot of your minutes:

> I talked with my parents, and they said I need to save my minutes. So now I can lend my phone only in emergencies. Sorry.

If a kid in class is always looking at your answers:

> (It's hard to know for sure what a student is looking at, so just casually move your paper out of view.)

A TIP

When you solve problems on your own, your confidence will soar. Start small, such as asking a friend to return a book she has borrowed, and then build your experience from there. Be brave. You won't regret it.

now or later?

It's not just *what* you say that matters but *when* you say it. Test your timing with the questions below.

1. You're in bed, it's late, and your mom's about to turn out the light. You need to ask her about tomorrow's schedule. You decide to ask . . .

   ☐ **Now**   ☐ Later

2. Your mom says you can invite Amy over this weekend, and you see her at the mall talking to Melinda. You decide to invite her over . . .

   ☐ **Now**   ☐ Later

3. You sit down to dinner and want to ask your dad about joining the youth orchestra—tryouts are next week. You decide to ask . . .

   ☐ **Now**   ☐ Later

4. You call your friend to tell her that you're going to New York City for spring break, and she tells you that her dad lost his job. You decide to tell her your news . . .

   ☐ **Now**   ☐ Later

5. Your sister's working on an important paper that's due. She's asked that you not interrupt, but her friend Brenna has called three times. You're not sure, but you decide to tell her . . .

   ☐ **Now**   ☐ Later

Answers

1. Now

It's late, so it may not be the time to get into a long discussion, but this is a quick question and time-sensitive, so it's fine.

2. Later

Unless you're inviting Melinda, too, best to talk about it in private. It would be OK to ask Amy to call you later, though.

3. Now

Dinner is the perfect time to discuss what's on your mind.

4. Later

Talking about your trip would make her feel even worse. Now is the time to comfort your friend, not brag about your good news.

5. Depends!

This isn't a trick question—it's a judgment call. Think it through, and make your choice based on what you know about your sister and her friend.

accepting gifts

A gift is just that—a gift. It's not something you get to choose. Whatever it is, accept the gift with a genuine "Thanks! That was so nice of you." Then, if it's an option, exchange the item for something else, or donate it and enjoy the gift of helping others.

But what if . . .

• your music teacher gives you a stuffed bear, and you're allergic to dust mites?

• your mom's friend buys you a shirt that's two sizes too small?

• your troop leader gives you a CD you already own?

• you're deathly afraid of bees, and your neighbor makes you a blanket with bumblebees all over it?

• your friend shows up with a big present on Valentine's Day, and you have only a card for her?

• your aunt sends you a stuffed dinosaur that teaches you how to count, and you're ten years old?

• your grandma gives you oversized underwear that you open up at your girl/boy party?

• you save up your allowance to buy your friend a sterling-silver charm bracelet, and she gives you a key chain from a dollar store?

It doesn't matter if the gift is cheap, wrong, ugly, over the top, or just plain ridiculous—if someone gives you a gift, you smile nicely and say . . .

when you're grateful

If someone goes out of her way to make you feel really special, look that person in the eye and sincerely thank her. Yeah, it'll take a bit of bravery, but the effort is worth the reward. She'll know that what she did meant the world to you.

If a classmate helps you pick up your papers after they fall everywhere:

> Thank you so much. I really mean it. You're a lifesaver.

If your "secret Santa" goes all out for your surprise:

> You really went the extra mile! A BIG thank you!

If your teacher spends 25 extra minutes after school teaching you long division until you finally understand it:

> Thanks for the extra help, Ms. Canvella. I know you're busy, and this was really helpful.

If a girl you don't know very well stands up for you when another student makes fun of your new jeans:

> Thanks for having my back. That was really cool, and I won't forget it.

If the school librarian remembers that you love horse books and hands you the latest one when you walk in the library:

This is awesome! Thanks for thinking of me. I'm going to read it right now.

If a boy in your class asks about your dad, who broke his leg skiing:

He's doing OK. Thanks for asking. That was really nice of you.

If your neighbor hands you a big jar of change so that you can give it to the charity you're trying to support:

Dr. MacDonald, that's so generous and means a lot to me. Thank you so much.

If your faraway friend's parents offer to drive her to see you so that the two of you can visit:

Are you sure? Wow! That's so nice of you to give up your weekend for us. I can't wait to see Natalie. This is amazing!

follow the signs

There is no ONE right way to say what's on your mind, but there are wrong ones. Pay attention to the signs that your communication is going in the wrong direction.

Stop
You'll know your conversation is heading in the wrong direction if you get an angry response. Change tracks.

Go Back
If you say the wrong thing, you need to go back and make it right.

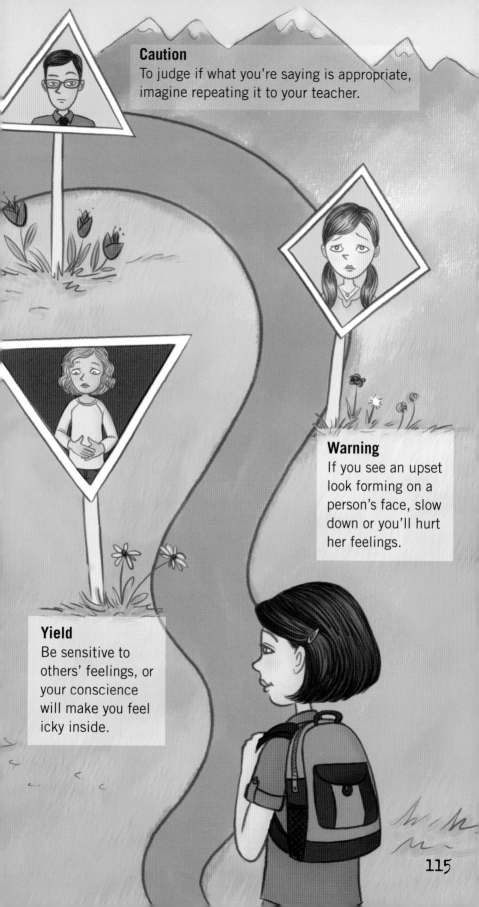

Caution
To judge if what you're saying is appropriate, imagine repeating it to your teacher.

Warning
If you see an upset look forming on a person's face, slow down or you'll hurt her feelings.

Yield
Be sensitive to others' feelings, or your conscience will make you feel icky inside.

115

how to know if you're a confident communicator

Read the questions below. If you can answer "yes" to a question, check that box. The more checks, the more confident you are about what you say and how you say it. Use the unchecked boxes as ideas for improving your communication skills.

☐ Do you smile, look straight into the eyes of the person you're speaking with, and use other nonverbal clues to show that you're open to communication?

☐ Do you speak from the heart, asking for and sharing information?

☐ Do you give and receive compliments freely and often?

☐ If you think that you've offended someone, do you quickly address the blunder and apologize?

☐ If you and a friend want different things, do you know how to compromise—to find a solution that works for both of you?

☐ Do you make others feel good about themselves?

☐ Do you let others know that it's OK to disagree?

☐ When someone hurts your feelings, do you take the time to think through your next move?

☐ Do you say what you mean, mean what you say, and say it without being mean?

it's magic!

You don't have to believe in magic to know that there are magic words. When you say these particular words with confidence and kindness, they magically make your message easier to hear. Magic words tell people that you respect them, and that makes the world a better place.

Do you know the magic words? Write them in the blanks.

1. If you request something, you say, _____ .

2. If someone performs even the smallest act of kindness, you acknowledge it with a _____ .

3. If you make a mistake, as an apology, you say, _____ .

4. If you need to interrupt or make way for yourself, you say, _____ .

5. If someone shows gratitude for something you did or said, you say, _____ .

Do you have a way with words?

Do you want to get in the last word?

Are you a person of many words?

Write to us! Send letters to:

A Smart Girl's Guide to Knowing What to Say Editor
American Girl
8400 Fairway Place
Middleton, WI 53562

Here are some other American Girl books you might like:

☐ I read it.

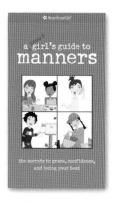

☐ I read it.

☐ I read it.

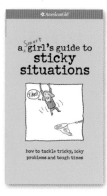

☐ I read it.

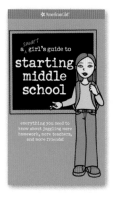

☐ I read it.

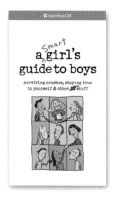

☐ I read it.